knowing when to leave

When staying in a relationship is costing too much

jace sterling

contents

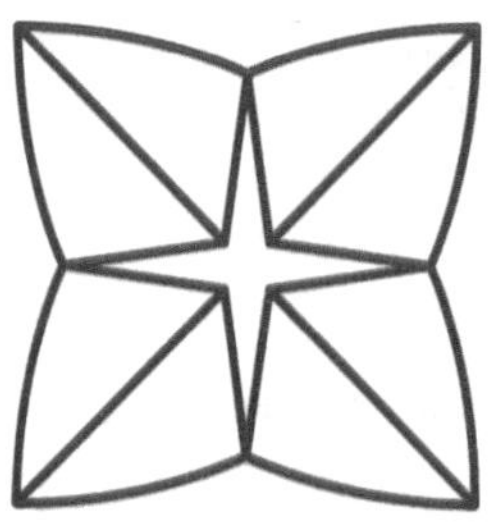

Knowing when to leave
ISBN: 978-1-7642017-6-6 paperback
ISBN: 978-1-7642017-3-5 e-book
© Jace Sterling 2026

First published in Brisbane, Australia, in 2026 by **Dare to Press Pty Ltd.**

Logo design by Scott Henderson
Printed and bound by an independent print-on-demand service.
Some identifying details have been changed to protect individual privacy.

disclaimer

This book is provided for general informational and educational purposes only. It is not intended to replace medical, psychological, legal, financial, or other professional advice.

The content reflects the personal experiences, perspectives, and observations of the author. Readers may wish to seek guidance from qualified professionals when making decisions that may affect their health, safety, relationships, finances, or legal circumstances.

To the fullest extent permitted by law, the author and publisher disclaim responsibility for any loss, injury, or damage arising from the use of this material.

introduction

This book is not here to persuade you to leave a relationship, and it is not here to convince you to stay. It will not tell you how to move on faster, how to repair what is breaking, or how to secure what comes next. It will not position you as broken, unfinished, or incapable of navigating this season in your own way.

> *It is here to sit with a particular moment. The moment when something inside your relationship has shifted in a way you can no longer easily dismiss. An awareness that may once have felt faint, but now feels harder to ignore.*

You may still love the person. You may still hope things will turn. You may have children, shared history, financial ties, promises that once felt unshakeable. You may have considered leaving before and decided not to. You may be tired of your own internal back and forth.

Realising something is no longer sitting right does not automatically bring clarity. Often it makes things feel more complicated. Conversations intensify. Negotiations deepen. You may try one more compromise, one more discussion, one more attempt to steady what feels unstable. And yet, underneath the effort, something continues to register, not dramatically, not loudly, just consistently.

You begin to notice the cost of continuing in the same way. The energy it takes. The adjustments required. The quiet override of your own instincts. Not because you do not care. Not because you have not tried. But because the arrangement as it stands no longer feels sustainable.

For some, this awareness builds slowly over years. For others, it arrives through exhaustion, illness, anxiety, or a moment of clarity that feels almost physical. However it comes, it has weight.

> *What follows is rarely neat. There can be grief, not only for the relationship, but for the version of yourself that existed within it. For the shared identity. For the imagined future. Even for the effort itself. Routine, intensity, closeness, tension, longing, all of it forms part of the structure you have been living inside. No one steps away without feeling the shift.*

Knowing when to leave is not about drama. It is not about proving a point. It is not about winning or being right. **It is about recognising when something has reached its natural limit, even if the shape of what comes next is still unclear.**

This book stays with that recognition. The pages that follow are reflections, observations of the quiet moments people move through when they are standing at this threshold.

If you find yourself here, you may already recognise some of what is forming.

how to use this book

You do not need to read this book in order, and you do not need to recognise yourself on every page. It is not something to complete or move through quickly. This book is designed to be dipped into, returned to, and set aside as needed.

The book is made up of **short segments.** Each one names a single, recognisable experience that can arise before, during, or after leaving a relationship. Some may feel immediately familiar. Others may not land at all. You may pause after a page, skip ahead to something that feels closer to where you are, or return to the same segment more than once. There is no expectation of continuity.

There is nothing here to apply, practise, or decide. The segments do not build toward an outcome, and they are not intended to move you forward or help you reach clarity. They simply describe moments that are often lived quietly, especially when they are still unfolding and hard to name.

Toward the back of the book, you will find **two optional sections.**

The **statistics section** is included for readers who find reassurance in scale and context. It exists to show how common separation and singlehood are across different stages of life. You can read it, skim it, or skip it entirely.

The rights list is a short permission based section. It does not tell you what to do. It simply names what many people already sense they are allowed to choose, but may not yet feel steady enough to claim.

If something in these pages feels recognisable, you can let it register without doing anything with it yet. If something does not resonate, you can leave it behind. Read in whatever way feels easiest, and take only what feels supportive to you right now.

1
when something
no longer sits right

when something feels off

It rarely begins with anything obvious.

There is no clear moment where you decide something is wrong. It arrives quietly. A mild tension that settles into the background of your days. You tell yourself it is stress, or tiredness, or just a phase. Relationships shift. People go through seasons.

And yet, a subtle tightening forms inside you. A hesitation before certain conversations. A small resistance that did not used to be there. You notice it, then override it.

There has been no betrayal, no explosion, no single event you can point to. Everything continues much as it always has. But inside, the arrangement no longer sits the way it once did.

You carry on. You show up. You function.

Beneath the routine, a quiet awareness begins to form. Not

panic. Not urgency. Just a sense that what you are feeling is not random.

You cannot fully name it yet. You only know that something has changed in a way that feels small, but persistent.

And once you become aware of that change, even faintly, it tends to return.

---

small disappointments add up

It begins to look less like a feeling and more like a pattern.

Not major breaches. Smaller repeats. Plans that slip more than once. A message left unanswered. A promise made lightly, then forgotten just as lightly. A tone that flattens when something matters to you.

Individually, each moment seems manageable. You tell yourself it is not worth escalating. It is easier to move past it and keep the day steady.

But you begin to notice how often follow through does not happen. How often repair only happens if you initiate it. How often you leave a conversation carrying the unfinished part alone.

Outwardly, nothing appears broken. Privately, you can list the moments.

The issue is not intensity. It is repetition.

You find yourself mentally tallying without meaning to. Not obsessively. Just quietly.

And one day, the tally feels clearer than the explanations.

It does not feel like a crisis.

It feels like evidence.

---

when you stop bringing it up

There is a point where you notice you are holding things back.

Not because the issue disappeared. Not because it stopped mattering. But because you are tired of what usually follows.

You think about raising something, then picture the conversation. The defensiveness. The familiar shift away from what you meant to say. You decide it is not worth it.

So you let it go.

At first, it feels sensible. Not everything needs to become a discussion.

But over time, the silence becomes deliberate.

You begin filtering what you share. Skipping detail. Softening reactions. Letting moments pass that once would have required clarity.

The relationship may appear smoother on the surface.

Privately, you notice how much of yourself stays unspoken.

relief when they're not home

There are moments when the house feels different because they are not in it.

The air is quieter. The pace shifts. You move through rooms without anticipating a reaction or adjusting your tone. You make small decisions without considering how they will land. The relief is subtle, but unmistakable.

At first, you frame it generously. Everyone needs space. Time alone is healthy. It is normal to enjoy a change in rhythm.

And that may be true.

But the feeling lingers longer than expected. It is not just rest. It is expansion. Your body settles in a way it does not when they are present. Your thoughts move more freely. You notice how little bracing is required.

When they return, nothing overtly wrong occurs. The routine resumes. Conversation fills the space. And yet, somewhere inside, something tightens again.

The relief was not about solitude.

It was about the absence of tension you had stopped noticing.

Once you feel that difference, even briefly, it is difficult to dismiss.

---

explaining away your discomfort

At first, you provide the explanation before anyone else needs to.

They were busy. They forgot. They are not good with occasions. It is not really about the gift.

When Christmas passes quietly, or Mother's Day feels like an afterthought, you minimise it. It does not need to become something bigger.

Sometimes they offer the explanation too. You are reading too much into it. It was just poor timing. They meant to do more.

You nod. It sounds reasonable enough.

When they are abrupt with your friend, you call it stress. When something that mattered to you is dismissed, it becomes miscommunication. The meaning is adjusted so it lands more softly.

Individually, each moment can be defended.

But it takes effort to keep reframing them.

You begin to notice how quickly you step in to reduce the impact. How easily the explanation replaces the feeling.

The discomfort does not disappear.

It simply changes form.

editing yourself mid-sentence

It does not always begin with silence.

Sometimes it begins with a sentence you almost finish.

You start to say what you mean, then feel the familiar shift before it even happens. You can already see where the conversation will go. The defensiveness. The detour. The way your point will be reframed into something you did not intend.

So you adjust.

A word softened. A detail removed. A sharper truth diluted before it leaves your mouth.

It is not that you have nothing to say. It is that you recognise the pattern. You have seen how this version of the argument unfolds, and how little it changes.

Sometimes you worry your words will be twisted. Sometimes you are simply too tired to repeat yourself.

So you choose the safer sentence.

The room stays steady. The conflict never fully forms.

They continue speaking, unaware of what you edited out.

And the absence of that recognition lands heavier than the argument you avoided.

---

the same conversation again

You recognise it before it fully begins.

A slight change in tone. A shift in posture. A sentence that opens in a way you have heard before.

You feel yourself brace, not dramatically, but instinctively.

The topic may be different. The words may vary. But the structure underneath remains the same. You raise something. It is redirected. Clarified into something else. Returned to you in a form you did not intend.

You try again, briefly. You adjust your phrasing. You narrow your point.

And then the turn arrives.

The focus shifts. The meaning tilts. The original thread slips quietly out of reach.

You have been here before.

There is a strange quality to it, almost surreal. You can see the loop forming while you are still inside it. You can see how it will end while it is still unfolding.

Eventually, the conversation settles back into its established rhythm.

The surface calms. The original point remains untouched.

Just the quiet recognition that this exchange has unfolded this way many times before.

---

managing their reactions

Over time, you become attentive to their temperature.

You notice the early signs. A tightening in their voice. A look that signals irritation. A shift in tone that suggests something is about to turn.

Without announcing it, you begin adjusting.

You phrase things carefully. You time conversations strategically. You soften observations that might land too directly. You choose moments when they seem most receptive.

It feels responsible at first. Considerate, even. Every relationship requires awareness of the other person.

But gradually, the awareness becomes vigilance.

You are scanning for signals before you speak. Weighing whether a topic is worth the reaction it may trigger. Calculating how to keep the atmosphere steady.

Sometimes the adjustment is subtle.

Other times, you realise you are working harder to maintain equilibrium than to express what you actually feel.

You are no longer simply participating in the exchange.

You are regulating it.

---

lonely while partnered

You can sit beside someone and still feel the distance.

Sometimes you try to close it.

You plan a day out. A family trip. A dinner meant to feel different. You tell yourself that a change of setting might soften whatever has been forming between you.

For a while, it almost works. The children are animated. The photos look easy. There are moments that resemble what once came naturally.

But as the day unfolds, you notice the quiet comparison running in the background.

The way it used to feel. The ease that did not require effort.

The way conversation once carried itself instead of needing encouragement.

On the drive home, the contrast settles in.

The day would appear ordinary enough.

There was no conflict. No raised voices. Nothing to explain.

And yet the bridge did not restore itself.

If anything, the effort outlined the gap more clearly.

You sit next to them, aware that something has shifted.

Not in loyalty. Not in appearance.

In access.

when your body knows first

Sometimes the first signal does not arrive as a thought.

It arrives in the body.

Your sleep shifts. You wake slightly braced. Your energy feels flatter than it used to. Small routines require more effort. You reach for comfort more often, or lose interest in things that once steadied you.

It is easy to explain these changes away.

You are getting older. Work is busy. Everyone is stretched. This is just what adulthood feels like.

And that may be true.

But the pattern has a context. Certain evenings feel heavier. Certain conversations leave a residue that lingers longer than expected. You notice habits adjusting quietly around that tension.

Daily life continues much as it always has.

Still, your system seems to be working harder than before.

Your thoughts may still be debating what is reasonable.

Your body is responding to what it is living inside.

Long before you call it misalignment, something in you has already registered the strain.

Not as a verdict.

As a signal.

2

the ways we stay

staying for the children

It can feel unthinkable to disrupt what the children know.

On an ordinary Tuesday night, the two of you are tired. There are lunches to pack, forms to sign, dishes in the sink. Even strained, the system works. If one of you is late, the other adjusts. If a child is sick, someone stays home. You think, if I were doing this alone, it would be heavier.

You look at their routines. Their bedrooms. The way they move easily between both of you. You imagine explaining something you are not yet ready to name.

You watch them laugh with the person you are struggling beside and it complicates everything. The tension between you does not always touch them directly. Not in ways they would describe.

You tell yourself that stability matters more than discomfort. That adulthood requires endurance. That you can carry what feels strained so they do not have to.

You begin weighing your private unease against their visible security.

The scale rarely feels simple.

So you stay a little longer.

Not because nothing is wrong.

But because changing it would rearrange more than just you.

---

staying because it is not that bad

There are relationships that are clearly destructive.

And then there are the others.

No shouting that carries through walls. No single event that demands action. The house runs. The bills are paid. The children are where they need to be.

It is not that bad.

The effort may not be equal, but it feels manageable. One of you carries more of the invisible work. The other assumes it will be done. At first, adjusting seems simpler than addressing it.

Over time, the friction shows up in small places. Dishes left in the sink. A tone that lands a little flat. A comment that lingers longer than it should.

There are still good days. Shared jokes. Practical teamwork.

You compare your situation to worse stories. You lower the threshold of what qualifies as unacceptable.

It functions.

Dinner is made. Homework is signed. The calendar fills.

Nothing collapses.

And that stability can be enough to keep everything in place.

---

hoping it will return to how it was

You remember the beginning.

The ease. The attention. The version of the two of you that felt aligned without effort. It is not fantasy. It existed.

So you hold onto it.

You tell yourself that this current version is temporary. That stress, children, work, fatigue have layered over something still intact underneath.

You notice small things that used to come naturally. A hand at the small of your back in the kitchen. A shared meal without distraction. A goodbye at the door that lingered a second longer. You tell yourself those gestures are simply buried, not gone.

You revisit old trips, old messages, old photographs. You use them as evidence.

If it was real once, it can be real again.

You believe that with the right tone, the right patience, the right adjustment, the earlier version might return.

It feels loyal to hope.

It feels premature to accept that something fundamental may have shifted.

So you give it more time.

And sometimes the memory of how it felt becomes stronger than the reality of how it does.

------

the fear of starting over

Leaving is not just emotional.

It is the unraveling of something you have already organised your life around.

You picture a different address. A different routine. Conversations that would have to be had more than once. You imagine telling people who assumed this was permanent.

You wonder what the quiet would feel like. Whether it would steady you or echo.

The relationship may be strained, but it is known. You understand its patterns. You know how to anticipate its shifts. You have learned how to move within it.

Starting over means stepping into variables you cannot predict. How you will feel in six months. Who you will become without this structure. Whether you will regret choosing disruption over familiarity.

Uncertainty can feel heavier than dissatisfaction.

So you delay the possibility.

You tell yourself that change should be certain before it is chosen. That clarity should arrive before action.

And when certainty does not arrive, staying begins to feel safer than risking what you cannot yet see.

---

protecting the shared history

You have built years together.

Photographs. Milestones. Private language no one else understands. Seasons that were hard and somehow survived.

People know you as a pair. Invitations arrive addressed to both of you. Your story is woven into family memory.

Leaving does not erase that history, but it changes how it is held.

You hesitate at the thought of reframing it. Of watching something that once felt formative be reduced to a chapter that ended.

There were real things here. Real laughter. Real effort. Real love at one point.

It feels unsettling to separate from that without diminishing it.

Part of you wants to honour what was good, even if what is happening now feels thinner.

History carries weight. Not all of it is broken.

Sometimes you remain not only because of the present, but because stepping away feels like rewriting something you once believed in.

And altering that story feels heavier than leaving it as it stands.

Financial Entanglement and Practical Fear (Refined)

There are numbers involved.

Mortgages. School fees. Shared accounts. Retirement plans. Insurance. Debt.

The life you built is not only emotional. It is contractual.

You begin to calculate quietly. What separation would mean in practical terms. Who would move. What would be sold. Whether one income is enough. Whether two households are possible.

The emotional strain may feel manageable. The financial implications are less abstract.

You open spreadsheets. You check balances. You imagine legal consultations instead of conversations.

It is not only about loneliness. It is about solvency. Stability. Predictability.

Disruption carries a price tag.

So you pause.

Not because nothing feels strained.

But because untangling it would require signatures, valuations, and new addresses.

The numbers sit there, waiting to be faced.

And you close the laptop for now.

loyalty to the promise you once made

You stood in front of people and said words you meant.

You believed them at the time.

The promise was not symbolic. It reflected who you were then, what you understood, and what you expected would unfold.

When the relationship begins to strain, those words do not vanish. They remain part of the structure.

Commitment once felt expansive and mutual. Clear in its direction.

Over time, people change. Circumstances shift. Capacity expands in some places and narrows in others. The version of you who made that promise is not identical to the person standing here now.

Acknowledging that can feel disorienting.

You may question whether stepping away diminishes what was real. Or whether it simply recognises that growth does not always move in parallel.

The promise still matters.

And the reality you are living inside does not disappear.

Holding both can create a quiet tension that does not resolve easily.

minimising your own needs

You begin adjusting quietly.

It is not that your needs disappear. They simply start to feel flexible.

Certain conversations matter less. Certain gestures become optional. Depth feels negotiable.

You scale your expectations to match what is consistently available.

You frame it as maturity. As realism. As understanding that no relationship provides everything.

It can feel responsible to reduce friction. Sensible to want less.

Over time, you become skilled at translating absence into adequacy. If something is not offered, you learn not to expect it. If something feels missing, you tell yourself it may not be essential after all.

You focus on what works. You emphasise what is functional. You adjust the definition of enough.

The shift is gradual.

It does not arrive with a clear boundary.

But the space you occupy begins to change shape around what you no longer ask for.

---

waiting for the right time

The decision is rarely avoided all at once.

It is managed.

You widen the conditions. You set new thresholds. You add one more variable that needs to settle before anything can change.

After this project. After the holidays. After things feel calmer. After one more proper conversation.

You look for signs of improvement and give them more weight than they might deserve. A good weekend becomes evidence. A softer tone becomes progress.

You adjust your own behaviour in the meantime. You speak more carefully. You initiate more often. You become more patient than you were before.

If something shifts slightly, you call it momentum. If it does not, you call it timing.

The question is not dismissed.

It is deferred.

The future becomes the place where clarity will arrive.

And in stretching the timeline, the present remains undisturbed.

---

telling yourself this is just what marriage is

You look around and see other couples who seem tired. Busy. Slightly disconnected.

You hear casual remarks about long term partnership losing

intensity. About romance softening into routine. About compromise becoming the baseline.

It begins to sound ordinary.

You compare what you feel to what appears common. You measure your dissatisfaction against jokes, anecdotes, and photographs that show only selected moments.

Perhaps this is adulthood. Perhaps this is how things settle after the early years. Perhaps wanting more ease or depth is naïve.

The thought steadies you.

If everyone adjusts, then adjustment must be maturity.

What feels thin becomes familiar. What feels distant becomes standard. The absence of spark is reframed as stability.

Nothing appears broken. It simply looks like longevity.

And in calling it normal, the question of whether it still fits you becomes easier to set aside.

3

the cost of continuing

navigating around tension

It does not begin with arguments.

It begins with adjustments.

You learn the contours of what will tip a mood. You choose when to raise something and when to let it go. You delay plans until the timing feels safer. You rehearse how a conversation might land before you start it.

Sometimes you plan in advance to prevent friction. Other times you avoid planning at all because that, too, can create it.

You begin shaping the day around what will keep things even.

You suggest an outing carefully. You hold back an idea if it feels likely to be dismissed. You decide it is easier not to push for what you want than to navigate the reaction that might follow.

None of it feels dramatic.

It can even feel cooperative. As though you are both working quietly to keep the peace.

But the process is deliberate.

Spontaneity narrows. Certain topics thin out. Decisions become more strategic than natural.

Before long, the relationship feels less like something you move through freely and more like something you move around carefully.

***

carrying more than you should

When things begin to strain, someone keeps the day intact.

You answer the emails.

You make the lists.

You remember the dentist appointment and the form that needs signing.

You show up to work as if nothing at home is fraying.

It is not that you feel steady.

It is that stopping is not an option.

You tell yourself you will do what it takes. That if you carry more, the strain might settle. That this phase will eventually move.

So you stretch.

You take on the extra tasks.

You absorb the tension.

You keep the routines running.

The arguments do not disappear.

They simply feel unproductive.

Explaining how overwhelmed you are requires energy you no longer have. Reaching for support risks being misunderstood, or met with another account of how difficult things are on the other side too.

So you keep going.

From the outside, you look capable.

Inside, you are carrying more than feels sustainable, holding more threads than you can comfortably manage.

Nothing visibly breaks.

But the sense of standing alongside someone, rather than alone, grows thinner.

resentment you do not voice

It does not arrive as anger.

It shows up in small pauses. In thoughts you keep to yourself. In the way a comment lingers longer than it should.

You notice irritation rising at things that once felt minor. A task left undone. A promise loosely kept. A tone that suggests you are overreacting.

You consider saying something.

Sometimes you begin to.

But you weigh the likely response. The explanation that will follow. The familiar circularity. You decide it is not worth reopening.

So the irritation has nowhere to go.

It does not disappear. It settles.

You carry it quietly through the rest of the day. It shapes how you respond, even when you are trying not to let it.

You are not explosive. You are not confrontational.

You are simply holding something that never fully clears.

And over time, you begin to recognise the feeling more quickly than the event that triggered it.

---

when your world becomes smaller

You begin opting out quietly.

An invitation feels heavier than it used to. A weekend away seems complicated. You consider the conversation that might follow, the coordination required, the energy it will take to re-enter your own home afterward.

So you stay.

You tell friends you are busy. You shorten phone calls. You let certain connections thin without formally ending them.

The relationship occupies more of your internal space than it once did. Even when you are elsewhere, part of you is tracking it. Monitoring tone. Anticipating shifts. Managing what will need attention later.

There are still outings. Still shared events. Nothing that signals withdrawal.

But you notice how much of your time now moves between responsibility and recovery.

There is less room for anything beyond what is already being managed.

Not because you decided to shrink your life.

Because maintaining it has become enough.

losing interest in explaining yourself

There are moments when your meaning does not land the way you intended.

You mention something in passing. It returns to you sharpened. You ask a practical question. It is heard as criticism. You follow up on an offer. Irritation meets you instead.

At first, you correct it.

You explain what you knew at the time. You outline what you were responding to. You fill in the missing context.

Sometimes you realise there was information you did not have. Sometimes the reaction seems to move ahead of what was actually said.

You adjust and try again.

Over time, the pattern becomes familiar.

Clarifying once feels sensible. Clarifying repeatedly feels heavier. You notice how often the conversation bends in the same direction, regardless of your explanation.

So you simplify.

You answer with fewer details. You stop revisiting certain exchanges. You allow some distortions to pass without defending yourself.

The explanations grow shorter.

The effort to correct the meaning no longer feels necessary.

---

anxiety that feels disproportionate

Sometimes the reaction arrives louder than the moment requires.

A small oversight. A forgotten form. A bill paid late. The situation is manageable. You know it is manageable.

Still, your response comes quickly.

Your voice tightens. Your thoughts accelerate. The inconvenience feels heavier than it objectively is. You speak more sharply than you intended. You outline consequences that stretch further than the event itself.

Even as you are responding, part of you notices the scale does not match.

You tell yourself to lower it.

The body does not follow.

It is not the single incident that carries the weight. It is the accumulation behind it. The conversations that did not resolve. The responsibilities that did not redistribute. The steady effort required to keep everything functioning.

The current moment becomes the outlet.

From the outside, it can look like overreaction.

Inside, it feels like overflow.

When the tension has been running high for long enough, even ordinary disruptions begin to land as if they are larger than they are.

Not because the event is extreme.

Because your margin is thin.

the emotional hangover after conflict

The conversation ends.

No raised voices. No sharp exits. You return to the evening as planned. Dishes are washed. Messages are answered. The house settles.

But something in you does not.

Hours later, you are still replaying a sentence. The tone. The look that followed. What you meant to say. What you decided not to.

You tell yourself it was minor. It happens. And in the moment, that may even be true.

Yet your body remains slightly alert. Your shoulders stay lifted. Your thoughts circle back when you would rather be resting.

By morning, the topic is technically closed.

But the feeling lingers.

It is not the disagreement itself that stays with you. It is the after-effect. The way your body does not quite return to neutral. The way a small exchange continues quietly in the background of the next day.

You begin to notice how often the evening ends, and still, something inside you remains slightly unsettled.

when your standards quietly lower

It is not always a conscious shift. You begin to notice the space between what you reach for and what meets you. A story you share receives a brief reply. A hard day is acknowledged but not entered into. A gesture you once expected no longer arrives.

Nothing overt is wrong. There are still routines, shared logistics, familiar patterns. But something that once felt mutual now feels uneven.

You sense it in small moments. Sitting beside each other, you feel the difference between presence and proximity. You speak and notice when the exchange ends sooner than it once did. You wait, briefly, for something more. Often, it does not come.

Gradually, you stop anticipating what rarely arrives. You adjust in advance. You ask for less. The gap does not disappear, but your expectations narrow around it.

You continue functioning inside the relationship, quietly aware that what you need and what consistently arrives are no longer aligned.

And over time, that quiet adjustment begins to shape how much you trust your own sense of what you require.

4

the decision
before the decision

the thought you do not say out loud

It rarely arrives during an argument or a dramatic moment. More often, it forms in something ordinary. Driving home. Folding laundry. Sitting beside them while the television runs.

The thought surfaces quietly. You do not say it. You do not test it aloud. You let it pass once, then notice when it returns. It is not a plan, not a decision. It is a sentence you do not complete.

What would it look like if I did not stay.

You do not attach timelines. You do not begin researching options. You do not tell a friend. You simply register that the idea no longer feels impossible to think.

For a long time, the possibility may have felt unthinkable. Now it feels available. Not urgent. Not dramatic. Just present.

You continue the evening as usual. You respond to questions. You discuss logistics. The routine holds. Beneath it, the thought remains. You do not push it forward, and you do not force it away.

It rests there, quiet but clear.

---

imagining life alone

The thought moves from abstract to practical.

You begin picturing ordinary details. Where you would live. Which side of the bed would feel unfamiliar. How mornings might unfold without negotiation.

You calculate quietly. Rent. School drop-offs. Weekends. The cost of two households instead of one. You imagine telling your child where they will sleep on certain nights. You picture the first evening alone in a different space.

The images are not dramatic. They are logistical.

Some feel manageable. Others feel heavier.

You notice which parts you focus on. The quiet. The relief of not navigating certain conversations. The weight of carrying everything yourself.

You do not share these rehearsals. They remain internal.

At times, the imagined version feels calmer than your current one. At other times, it feels uncertain.

You are not choosing yet.

You are mapping.

And in mapping it, the future feels less distant than it once did.

---

testing the idea privately

The thought does not remain abstract. You begin trying it on in small, contained ways.

You let a conversation about the future pass without reinforcing it. You answer a question about your relationship more neutrally than before. When someone assumes things are steady, you do not rush to confirm it. You notice how that feels.

You attend a school event alone and do not explain the absence. You make a decision about the weekend without checking first. You sit in a café or a cinema by yourself and register the quiet without filling it. None of it is an announcement. None of it is a plan.

It is rehearsal at the edges.

You observe your own response. Does the space feel unsettling? Does it feel steadier than expected? You notice the response without deciding what it means.

The idea moves through an ordinary day with you. You see whether it fades or returns. You are not leaving yet. You are noticing which version of your life feels easier when no one else is asking you to account for it.

---

the moment you stop defending the relationship

For a long time, you found explanations easily.

If someone questioned a comment, you clarified it. If a story sounded unbalanced, you added context. If a friend looked uncertain after hearing something, you reassured them. You protected the relationship from being misunderstood.

You told yourself that every partnership has private layers, that what others saw was only a portion.

A remark is made and you let it stand. Someone asks if things are difficult and you do not rush to soften the answer. A silence stretches where you might once have filled it.

You do not add criticism. You do not offer detail. You are simply no longer working to preserve the image.

It is a small shift, but you feel it.

The reflex to justify weakens. The urgency to balance the story recedes. You are not trying to turn anyone against the relationship. You are just no longer protecting it from scrutiny.

And in that quiet withdrawal of defence, the distance becomes harder to ignore.

when you notice you are done trying

There was a time when you kept looking for ways to repair things. You suggested conversations. You proposed small adjustments. You revisited the same issue from different angles, hoping one version might land more clearly than another. Even when the response felt partial, you tried again.

At some point, the impulse shifts.

The next time something goes unresolved, the energy to reopen it does not gather in the same way. You see the familiar pattern forming and do not step forward to interrupt it.

It is not dramatic. There is no announcement that you are finished. The effort simply does not rise as it once did.

You still participate, answer, and continue to show up, but the search for a breakthrough has lessened, and the urgency that once demanded your attention no longer carries the same weight.

You are no longer trying to make it into something else.

quiet clarity that does not need witnesses

At some point, the internal debate grows quieter.

You are no longer rehearsing both sides with the same intensity. The reasons to stay and the reasons to leave no longer trade places every hour. The back-and-forth slows.

The clarity does not arrive as a surge or demand to be spoken. It sits steadily beneath your daily routines.

You feel less need to gather agreement. There is no impulse to test the thought repeatedly with friends or build a case around it.

The understanding is quiet. It is simple.

When something happens that once would have sent you into analysis, the response is measured. You see it and recognise it.

The question no longer feels as open as it once did.

And that awareness stands on its own.

grieving before anything has ended

Formally, everything remains in place. The routines continue. The house runs. Conversations still take place.

And yet, something feels altered.

You find yourself noticing moments that carry a different weight. A shared joke that lands more softly. A familiar routine that feels less anchored. You watch an ordinary interaction and register a brief, unexpected sadness.

It is not constant. It comes in fragments.

You realise you are already missing something that has not technically gone. Not necessarily the relationship as it is now, but what it once represented. The version of the future you had assumed would unfold.

You hold certain memories with more care. Some evenings feel marked in a way they did not before.

You are not saying goodbye.

But part of you understands that something is shifting, even if it has not been declared.

And that understanding lingers.

---

the fear of being wrong

Clarity does not remove consequence. Even when the internal argument has quieted, the external implications remain.

You begin to think beyond the feeling and into the structure. Children who would move between homes. Finances that would need dividing. Property that cannot be separated without negotiation. Routines that would shift in ways no one can fully predict. The unknown is not abstract. It has names, dates, and forms to sign.

You consider how the other person might respond. Whether they will remain steady or become someone you have not seen before. Whether conversations will stay contained or widen into something harder.

The fear centres on initiating a change that cannot easily be reversed. You wonder if you are about to fracture something that, while imperfect, is still functioning. You wonder if staying would have been simpler, quieter, less disruptive.

The weight of that possibility can slow you. It can hold you in place longer than you expected.

The stakes are real, and once certain conversations begin, they do not return to where they started.

---

the fear of being right

Being wrong carries risk. Being right carries confirmation.

If you are wrong, there is still room to repair. A misunderstanding can be corrected. A difficult season can pass. The structure can hold.

If you are right, what you have been sensing may not change. The distance may not close. The patterns may not soften with more effort.

That possibility is harder to sit with.

It means acknowledging that the version of the relationship you hoped would return may not return in the way you once imagined. What feels misaligned may not be temporary.

You hesitate because confirming it would narrow your options.

You consider whether you could live with the truth as it stands, without trying to reshape it.

The fear is quiet. It is the fear that the clarity forming inside you may be accurate.

And if it is, then something you once believed in may not return to its earlier shape.

5

dismantling what was

telling them

After the conversation ends, the house does not immediately rearrange itself.

The furniture remains where it was. The hallway light still turns on. The evening continues in its usual sequence.

The reaction may be loud. Or restrained. Or uneven. It may stretch for hours, or fall into silence.

But once the words have been spoken, they remain in the room.

If you live together, you move around each other with new awareness. Doors close differently. Footsteps are noticed. Exchanges become practical.

Someone may leave. Or not. Someone may sleep elsewhere. Or remain in the same bed, both aware of the space between.

If you do not live together, the phone sits on the table without being picked up.

Ordinary tasks feel slightly altered. Washing a cup. Turning off a lamp. Locking the door.

There is no rehearsal now.

The words have been said.

And the space holds that fact while you move through it.

---

the first night apart

The first night apart has a physical quality that is difficult to ignore.

Whether the room is new or familiar, it does not register the way it once did. The layout may be known, but your orientation inside it feels altered. You move through the space with more attention than usual, aware of where things are, aware of yourself in relation to them.

The day has likely taken more out of you than you realised. Packing. Talking. Holding steady. Carrying what needs to be carried. Even if the day appeared controlled, the shift itself is effort.

When you are alone, the quiet feels different from other nights. It may be heavier. It may be sharper. It may simply feel unshared.

There may be relief in the absence of tension. There may be ache in the absence of presence. Both can sit in the same room.

You lie down and notice that your body does not fully settle. Because this configuration is different. Even if the walls are known, you feel slightly misplaced within them.

For a while, you remain aware of your own presence in the room.

practical conversations that feel unreal

The conversations shift to logistics.

You sit down and talk about dates. When the rent is due. Who will keep the spare key.

A number is checked. Written down. Checked again.

There is a pause over a bank transfer amount. One of you scrolls through a phone. The other waits.

You use ordinary planning language. "That works." "Let's confirm." "We'll need that in writing."

A detail is clarified. Then clarified again.

The discussion moves forward in small sections. One item at a time.

A calendar is opened. A date is entered. A reminder is set.

When the immediate points are covered, the conversation stops without ceremony. There are still other things to organise.

Later, you open your phone and see the reminder you set.

It sits there like any other appointment.

dividing objects that hold memory

When it comes time to divide belongings, the practical task rarely accounts for what the objects carry.

Some exchanges are calm. Others are tense. A question may be asked once or several times. An item may be offered quickly, claimed firmly, or set aside because neither of you wants to decide yet. The method varies. The fact of separation does not.

A photograph, a book, a lamp. Things that once felt simply shared now require ownership.

You pick something up and remember where it came from. The trip. The season. The version of you that chose it.

Some items feel heavier because of that. Some lose their place entirely. You may take something and later realise you do not want to live with what it stirs. Or leave something behind because carrying it feels like carrying more than the object itself.

By the end, the room looks altered. Not only because things have moved, but because they sit differently than they did before.

---

when logistics expand

In the weeks that follow, the practical layer grows.

Conversations narrow to arrangements. Access. Timelines. What stays. What moves. What needs to be confirmed.

How these exchanges unfold varies. Some are steady. Some abrupt. Some routed through others. You come to manage only your part.

There are moments when the discussion stays on task. There are others when tone shifts without warning. A message changes the direction of the day. A collection happens sooner than expected. An item is gone.

You return to the detail.

Dates are clarified. Documents located. A reminder set. An agreement recorded.

There are times when something larger rises underneath the surface of the conversation. You keep the focus where it is.

The work continues in small sections.

Outside of it, the rest of the day still requires attention.

The disentangling runs alongside everything else.

It does not resolve what is beneath it.

It simply moves what can be moved.

---

shared spaces becoming separate

After the separation, places do not disappear. They remain where they always were.

The café you both visited still opens at the same hour. The friend group continues to meet. Family events are still scheduled.

What changes is how you move through them.

Some invitations shift quietly. You attend on different days. You leave earlier than before. A familiar table feels less automatic. Some people are careful. Others are direct.

Certain places begin to feel layered. Not hostile. Not welcoming. Just altered. You are aware of who else might walk in. A street you once took together now carries an added calculation.

Other spaces open differently. You choose a new route home. Sit somewhere you would not have before. Try a place that was never "yours" as a couple.

You step into the same places, and they feel different in ways that are hard to name.

<hr>

explaining it to children

You choose a time when the house is quiet.

The table is cleared. The television is off. You sit down and place your hands flat against your knees so they do not move.

You begin with simple sentences. We have decided to live in different houses. You will spend time with both of us. Some things will stay the same.

You hear how deliberate your voice sounds. Slower than usual. Lower. You swallow before the second sentence and keep going.

You leave out the long conversations that led here. You do not revisit who said what. When your mind moves toward explanation, you return to the next short sentence instead.

There is a pause after each statement. You let it sit. You count a breath before speaking again.

They ask where they will sleep. You answer with the name of a suburb. You mention which nights.

You notice the urge to keep talking. To add context. You stop.

When the questions slow, you stand and carry the glasses to the sink. The dishwasher door clicks open. The evening continues.

---

when your name is said alone

After the first conversations, you begin to be addressed differently. Invitations arrive with one name instead of two. Introductions adjust. Seating arrangements shift without comment.

Sometimes the old version lingers. Someone refers to you collectively. A question assumes continuity. You correct it, or allow it to pass.

There are practical moments that carry more weight than expected. A form to update. An account still listed under a name you no longer feel connected to. A receptionist reading aloud a surname that no longer sits comfortably.

You respond. You clarify. You request the change, or decide not to in that moment.

Not every space requires explanation. Not every assumption is corrected.

Where there was once a pair, there is now a single name spoken.

You move through these adjustments one at a time.

---

uneven withdrawal

After the disclosure, the connection does not loosen all at once.

You still react. A comment lands sharply. An old argument surfaces and your body responds before you have time to moderate it.

Sometimes you lean in as if nothing has changed. You explain more than necessary. You offer reassurance you no longer intend to sustain.

Later, you notice it. The familiar pattern of offering more than the moment requires. Acting as though the arrangement is still intact.

Other times you pull back too quickly. You keep your tone short. You decline a request without softening it. You hold a boundary more rigidly than the moment calls for.

Neither response feels steady.

The instinct to repair is still there, but it no longer carries the same commitment. You step toward it, then away from it.

The adjustment is uneven.

You are no longer holding it together in the way you once did.

But you have not yet fully stopped responding to it either.

the pause you do not plan

Mechanism: Involuntary pause inside ongoing dismantling

The process does not finish neatly. There are still boxes along the wall. Messages unanswered. Lists forming quietly in your head. Something always remains mid-way.

But at some point, your body slows before the tasks do.

You sit down without deciding to. Or remain standing in the kitchen longer than necessary. The next thing to do is visible. You simply do not reach for it yet.

The momentum that carried you through conversations, arrangements, packing, decisions does not sustain itself indefinitely. It drops. Not dramatically. Just enough that continuing feels momentarily out of reach.

The room is not orderly. The work is not complete.

There is a stretch of time where you cannot plan the next move. Not because it does not exist. Simply because you do not move toward it.

You may lie back on a bed still surrounded by half-opened boxes. Or close your eyes in a chair while the house remains mid-transition.

The list continues in the background. You know it will resume.

For now, you stay where you are.

6
the emotional landscape after leaving

grief and relief existing together

In the early days after leaving, feeling rarely moves in a single direction. Relief may appear first, quietly, in practical ways. You choose what to watch. You sit where you like. You make a decision without negotiating it. The absence of tension can feel like oxygen returning to a closed room.

Then something unsettles it. You hear they are struggling with something ordinary, or your child mentions that the house feels different. Relief tightens. Concern rises without asking permission. Care does not disappear simply because the relationship has ended.

You may feel steadier than before and still find yourself wondering whether they are managing. The impulse to reach out can sit alongside the instinct to hold your boundary. Acting on one does not silence the other.

At the same time, guilt may flicker. Fear about money or

stability surfaces. Doubt appears without cancelling clarity. The emotions overlap.

Relief does not erase care. Care does not undo the separation. It is possible to feel lighter and heavier in the same week, sometimes in the same hour. Nothing lines up neatly.

missing them and not wanting them back

You might not miss the relationship as it was at the end. But you can still miss parts of the person.

It can happen unexpectedly. You see something they would have liked. A plant they would have insisted on buying. A joke they would have delivered perfectly. For a moment, you remember the version of them that felt warm, animated, familiar.

That memory can pull you closer.

And sometimes nothing immediately corrects it. The warmth can sit there for a while. An hour. A day. You may find yourself leaning into it before anything else surfaces.

Then, at some point, something else returns. A tone you used to brace for. A pattern you worked hard to manage. A way you felt smaller than you wanted to be.

Both recollections can exist together, even if they do not arrive at the same time.

What you felt may have been real for you, even if the dynamic was complicated.

The feeling rises. Then it settles.

You can sit with the tenderness and still recognise that it belongs to something finished.

the pull toward one more conversation

After leaving, there can be a sense that something remains unfinished. Not the logistics. Not the belongings. The words.

Certain exchanges replay. A sentence you wish you had clarified. An accusation you never answered. A moment where you felt misunderstood. The conversation may be over, but your mind continues it.

The urge to reach out often grows from that space. Not because you want the relationship restored, but because you want it settled. You imagine explaining yourself more clearly. Being heard without interruption. Having the ending acknowledged.

You might draft the message. Adjust the tone. Delete it. Rewrite it. Picture how they would respond.

And then you sit with the possibility that they may not respond as you hope. Or that the clarity you are seeking may not arrive at all.

Not every ending comes with mutual understanding. Sometimes the conversation continues only on your side.

The discomfort can linger. It does not disappear simply because contact has stopped.

the urge to reach out

That impulse does not always mean you want them back.

Sometimes it begins with something small. A detail you cannot locate. A task you used to leave to them without thinking. Over time, certain responsibilities settle into place. One of you keeps track of the documents. One of you manages the bookings. One of you steadies things when they tilt.

When that structure disappears, the gap shows up quickly.

Other times it arrives late at night. The house is still. Something unsettled moves through you and your hand reaches for your phone before you have decided why.

It may be your ex. It may be someone else. Someone familiar. Someone likely to answer.

The message can look practical. Or casual. Or harmless.

The phone is in your hand.

You pause.

The quiet feels heavier when there is no one else holding part of it.

doubting yourself in the quiet

After the separation, there is no automatic buffer.

If something shifts, you are the one who adjusts. A payment due. A schedule change. A decision that cannot wait. The responsibility does not circulate. It settles.

The doubt that surfaces is quieter than regret. It is about capacity.

Can you carry what arrives, without deferring it. Can you meet what is ordinary, and what is not.

The scale varies. For some, it is logistical. For others, financial. For others still, emotional. Whatever form it takes, there is no longer a shared default to absorb it.

The consequence rests with you.

You move through what arrives. You handle what can be handled. You leave what cannot be solved immediately where it is.

The exposure is steady. It does not argue with your choice. It simply requires you to stand inside the arrangement you now hold.

when the past feels different

With distance, memory rarely keeps every detail intact.

The sharpest moments can lose their edge. The tension, the fatigue, the small frictions that once felt constant no longer feel as immediate. What returns more easily are earlier scenes, lighter ones, where things seemed easier, or at least less strained.

For some, it moves in the opposite direction. The difficult exchanges grow larger in hindsight. The tenderness recedes. The story becomes clearer, but also harder.

Over time, the complexity can narrow. A whole relationship

begins to feel defined by a handful of dominant impressions, either warm or painful.

Certain details begin to rise first. Others fade further back.

The fuller texture does not disappear. It simply becomes harder to reach.

Memory can simplify what was once layered.

And that simplified version can begin to feel complete.

anger that arrives late

In the early stages, anger is often restrained. Not because it is absent, but because it could make things worse. Conversations need to remain measured. Shared responsibilities are still in motion. You understand how quickly anger can escalate something already fragile, so you contain it.

Later, when distance grows and the immediate consequences ease, something shifts. A memory lands differently. A moment you once minimised feels sharper. A pattern you adjusted around reads more clearly when you are no longer inside it. You begin to notice where keeping the peace required you to quiet parts of yourself.

The anger is not always loud. It can appear as firmness. Fewer explanations. Shorter responses. A steadier tone. What changes is not volatility, but access. The feeling is no longer deferred.

For some, anger turns inward as regret. Regret for what was accepted. For where you stayed quiet. For how easily your needs were folded into someone else's. For others, it turns outward into blame. Sometimes it does neither. It moves through quietly as clarity, then settles.

It does not have to become confrontation. Often it is simply the recognition that what once felt tolerable no longer does.

---

letting sadness move without escalation

Sadness after separation is rarely linear. You may feel steady for weeks, then something small unsettles you. A comment passed along. A story retold differently than you remember it. A moment that makes it clear you are no longer seen the way you once were. The hurt is not only about the relationship ending. It is about realising that the version of you that lived inside that relationship is no longer shared in the same way.

These moments can sting more than expected. Not because everything is collapsing again, but because they touch something tender. The urge to correct the record or explain yourself can be strong. To make sure what is being said feels fair.

Sometimes you choose not to. Not because it does not matter, but because stepping back protects your energy. There is sadness in allowing yourself to be misunderstood. There is also steadiness in recognising that not every version of events needs your pursuit.

The feeling may rise unexpectedly. You can acknowledge it without turning it into a battle. Sometimes letting the sadness exist, without escalation, is enough.

feeling lighter without celebration

Mechanism: Reduction of internal strain without emotional resolution

At some point, the internal pressure begins to soften. Not dramatically, and not in a way that invites announcement. You wake one morning and notice you are not bracing in the same way. The constant negotiation in your head is quieter. You are not replaying conversations before sleep or rehearsing how to manage the next one. The background effort that once ran through each day is no longer constant.

Nothing externally has become simple. There are still logistics, still conversations, still uncertainty. Grief has not disappeared. And yet something has shifted. You are no longer trying to make it hold together, and you are no longer adjusting yourself to fit back into it. What once required steady management is no longer shaping every moment.

It does not feel like celebration. It feels more like space. An evening passes without mental tallying. A conversation ends and does not follow you into the night. The absence of strain can feel unfamiliar, and you may even find yourself searching for what used to occupy that space.

There is no sudden joy and no sense of arrival. Only the quiet recognition that something heavy is no longer being carried in quite the same way. For now, that shift is simply noticeable.

7

quiet stabilisation

making room for yourself

At some point, something inside you begins to ask for space.

It does not arrive as a plan. It shows up as a preference you might once have dismissed. A piece of music you used to love. A class you once thought about taking. A pair of shoes you never quite justified buying. A comfort you postponed because other needs felt more pressing.

This time, you do not brush past it. You pause and let yourself consider it properly. You follow the thread a little further. The old songs play all the way through. You look up the class. You try something on. You book the haircut. You price the trip. You open the old diary. You sit longer than you intended.

You choose something because it feels right to you, not because it fits the mood of the room or keeps anyone else steady.

The day continues. There are still things to manage. But you notice that you are present in the decision in a way you were not before.

You stay with the feeling long enough to recognise it as yours.

---

returning to your own rhythm

For a while, your days still carry the imprint of the relationship.

You wake at the time that once worked for both of you. You plan around patterns that no longer need to exist. You adjust automatically, sometimes without noticing that you are still arranging your life around a shared tempo.

Then something begins to shift.

It might be practical. You book the gym at a time that suits you, even if it complicates someone else's expectations. You move an appointment. You see a friend on a night that used to be reserved. The change may create tension. Someone may question it. You feel that tension. You weigh it. Sometimes you keep the change.

Other adjustments are quieter. You return to a morning walk you once loved. You try an evening class. You restart something that fell away. Some of it fits. Some of it doesn't. You adjust again.

Gradually, your day begins to feel less organised around old patterns and more around what fits now. The rhythm is still forming. It may create friction. It may surprise you.

But it is becoming recognisably yours.

making a decision without consultation

There comes a moment when you change something in your space without asking anyone what they think.

It might be as simple as repainting a wall, replacing the curtains, moving the bed, or buying the chair you have always liked. The decision is not strategic or negotiated. You do not rehearse how you will justify it. You choose it because it feels right to you, and that is reason enough.

When the change is made, the room can feel different in a way that is hard to explain. Not better in a competitive sense, and not finished. Just more aligned. You look around and recognise yourself in it. The colour, the light, the arrangement reflects your taste without apology. There is no merged preference in the background, no quiet calculation about whether it will suit someone else.

Living inside that choice can feel grounding. The space starts to feel set up for you, instead of adjusted around someone else. It may still be imperfect. It may still evolve. But there is steadiness in knowing that this version of the room exists because you chose it.

You come home to it, and something in you settles.

the silence of your own routine

There comes a point when being alone no longer feels like something you are bracing for.

In the earlier stages, the quiet can feel exposed. When there is no one else in the room, everything inside you can seem louder. Questions surface. Old conversations replay. The space can feel as though it is asking something of you.

Over time, that intensity begins to ease. Evenings soften. You move through your routine without the same internal urgency. You make something to eat, or order in, or put music on simply because you feel like it. You sit down without scanning for what needs attention. The room does not press against you. It holds.

There is a steadier quality to your own company now. You are not trying to resolve anything. You are not trying to become someone different. You are simply present. The background sense that something is missing or unfinished begins to loosen.

These moments of calm start to feel more familiar.

Being alone with yourself begins to feel less like an absence and more like a place you can stand.

withdrawing energy without announcement

At some point, you notice you are no longer extending yourself in the same way. There is no formal decision and no need to mark the shift. It happens gradually, in how you respond and what you stop taking responsibility for. You answer what is asked without scanning ahead for the reaction. You let a message sit until you are ready to reply. You stop adding reassurance that was never requested, or cushioning statements before anyone has even misunderstood you.

Where you once filled pauses or softened tension before it formed, you begin to leave more space. If something is unclear, you may clarify once, but you do not keep circling back to secure agreement. If a comment carries an edge, you do not automatically smooth it over. The exchange becomes simpler because you are doing less extra work around it.

For some, this is the moment a quiet obligation loosens, especially if you were used to carrying more than your share of the emotional steadiness. For others, it is just the natural separation of two lives, even when there are still shared commitments that keep you in contact.

What remains feels less entangled, less anticipatory, and closer to your own lane.

allowing people to misunderstand you

There comes a point where you realise you cannot control how your story is carried by others. Pieces travel without context, events are summarised, and motivations are assigned. Some people ask questions. Others draw conclusions quietly.

You feel the impulse to correct it, to add the missing detail, to rebalance what feels uneven. Sometimes you do clarify, especially where it truly matters. But not every version requires your participation. Each defence extends the exchange, and each explanation invites another response.

Staying inside that loop can keep you tied to something you are trying to loosen.

For some, the misunderstanding feels sharp, particularly when relationships around you shift in tone. For others, it is more subtle, a quiet awareness that you are no longer fully seen in the way you once were. You weigh what engaging would cost, the energy, the reopening, the slow drift back into justification. Stepping back does not mean you agree with what is being said. It may simply mean you are no longer willing to keep the exchange alive.

Being fully understood by everyone may not be possible in this season. Staying steady within yourself may matter more. The misunderstanding may remain, and you may decide not to chase it.

standing on your own side

There are moments when something rises in you that feels uncomfortable. A reaction. A memory. A flicker of regret. Earlier, you might have moved quickly to analyse it, to correct it, or to decide what it meant about you. You might have replayed the scene in detail, adjusting your role inside it, searching for the point where you could have done better.

Standing on your own side can begin as a quieter shift. A memory surfaces and you notice it, but you do not automatically dive in. A feeling tightens and you let it be present without demanding that it resolve. You allow yourself to feel unsettled without assuming you are entirely at fault.

This does not mean you avoid reflection. It means you choose when to engage with it. Not every recollection requires a verdict. Not every discomfort requires a conclusion.

Over time, the relationship occupies less mental territory. When fragments return, they pass through more easily. You are not required to reopen the whole story each time.

You remain with yourself long enough to recognise that you do not have to rewrite your role in every memory in order to remain steady.

not wanting to go back

There comes a stage when returning no longer feels like something you are actively weighing. The shift is subtle but steady. You understand more clearly what that dynamic required from you and what it quietly cost over time.

You begin to see the pattern with less distortion. How often you overrode your own instinct. How easily you absorbed discomfort. How naturally you adjusted in order to keep things workable. It becomes harder to ignore the structure you were functioning inside, and the version of yourself that kept it running.

With that awareness, the idea of reentering something similar feels different. The comfort you once associated with it now sits alongside a clearer memory of the contraction. The cost is no longer abstract. You recognise it in practical terms, in energy, in attention, in the subtle ways you moved away from your own centre.

The thought of returning no longer pulls in the same way.

Something in you relaxes away from it instead of leaning back toward it.

8
after the weight shifts

when urgency fades

There was a period when everything felt as though it required resolution. Conversations lingered in your mind long after they ended, and questions pressed for answers. Even quiet evenings carried the sense that something still needed to be understood before you could properly rest.

Over time, that pressure begins to ease. A memory can surface without demanding investigation. A loose thread appears and you allow it to remain loose. You no longer feel compelled to revisit every exchange in search of a final interpretation. The relationship is no longer something that needs solving, and it no longer organises your present moment in the way it once did.

You may still think about it, and certain moments may still carry weight, but the thinking is no longer urgent. It does not insist on clarity before the day closes, and it does not require you to reach a verdict about who was right or wrong. Some questions remain unanswered, and you find that this no longer unsettles you in the same way.

What happened is part of your history, but it no longer feels like unfinished business. The pressure to resolve it has receded, and you move through the day without the quiet sense that something still needs to be settled.

no longer rehearsing conversations

There was a time when your thoughts would circle back without invitation. You replayed exchanges in detail, adjusting your wording and imagining how you might say it differently now. A sentence would return while you were driving or folding laundry, and you would quietly refine it, as though clarity could still be secured after the fact.

You also spent energy anticipating what might happen next. You pictured running into them somewhere unexpected. You imagined questions you hoped would not be asked. You shaped responses in advance, not because you were certain what would unfold, but because staying ahead of it felt safer than being caught unprepared.

Over time, something shifts almost without announcement. You notice one afternoon that you have not revisited the same exchange in days. A memory surfaces while you are making coffee or watching rain gather on the window, and instead of building a better version of it, you let it pass. An imagined conversation begins to form and then dissolves before it turns into a script.

It is not that awkward moments disappear. You still expect that something may land wrong or sting unexpectedly. But there is a growing tolerance for meeting it as it arrives. The present moment holds more space, and you move through your days without constantly preparing for conversations that are not actually happening.

seeing the relationship clearly

Earlier, your view of the relationship could tilt in different directions. On some days, you returned to what was lost, replaying moments of closeness as though they carried more weight than everything that followed. On other days, the strain felt dominant, as if the difficulty had defined the entire story. The memory shifted quietly with your mood.

Gradually, that swing begins to settle. The warmth and the difficulty start to sit alongside each other without competing for space. The ending no longer erases the beginning, and the beginning no longer excuses the end. You can acknowledge that there were parts that felt steady and parts that did not, without one cancelling the other.

What changes is not the past, but the scale. The relationship feels more proportioned in your mind. You recognise what worked for a time and what eventually did not. You see where you adapted, where you held on, and where there were limits that could not be negotiated. The exaggerations ease, and the minimising fades.

Sometimes that steadier view extends slightly outward. You notice familiar tendencies in yourself, the roles you slip into, the kind of closeness you hope for, and the ways you try to keep something balanced when it begins to tilt. Not as a judgement, and not as a plan for what comes next, just as something that is clearer than it once was.

The relationship remains part of your history, with its texture intact. It no longer shifts shape to match the emotion of the day, and it no longer requires you to defend or diminish it in order to feel steady.

accepting what is

For a long time, part of you may have continued to negotiate with what happened. Not always out loud, and not always in obvious ways, but quietly. You returned to certain turning points and imagined them unfolding differently. You reconsidered conversations, wondering whether a different tone might have altered the direction. Even after the decision was made, some part of you kept adjusting the pieces.

Over time, that negotiation begins to slow. The past remains unchanged, but it no longer feels like something you are actively trying to reshape. The outcome is not reinterpreted each week. The alternative versions grow less persuasive. You stop looking for the exact sentence that would have saved it, or the precise moment where you might have redirected it.

Accepting it leaves room for disagreement with how everything unfolded. Certain aspects may still feel unfair or unfinished. But the resistance softens. The relationship is no longer an argument you are trying to win inside your own mind.

It becomes something that happened. It had a beginning, a

middle, and a close. It carried warmth and strain. It reached a limit.

The internal struggle with that limit eases. You no longer need to correct the story in order to live alongside it.

letting the story simplify

There was a time when the story required detail. When someone asked what happened, you felt the need to explain it carefully. You included context. You clarified timing. You made sure the nuance was understood. Even in your own mind, the narrative unfolded in layers, with scenes and turning points arranged in sequence.

Over time, the story begins to contract. It is not that it was simple or unimportant, but that you no longer need every piece to be held up for inspection. When it comes up, you find yourself speaking about it more briefly. The outline is enough. The explanation does not stretch across the entire evening.

Internally, something similar happens. The relationship is no longer revisited in full detail. It becomes one chapter among others. You remember it when it is relevant, but you do not carry the full arc with you through each day.

The complexity remains intact. The texture is still there if you choose to look at it. But it no longer requires expansion in order to feel legitimate. The story settles into a shorter form, not because it has been reduced, but because it no longer needs to prove what it meant.

when it becomes your life

By the time you reach this point, life has already rearranged itself in quiet, practical ways. New routines have formed. The cupboards hold different things. The evenings unfold differently than they once did. You have learned how to carry what needs carrying. You have found your way through conversations you once feared, decisions you once postponed, moments you once thought might undo you.

There is something steady about that.

Singlehood, here, is not an argument and not a reaction. It is simply the life you are living now. You move through it in your own rhythm. You make choices and live with what they bring. You begin to notice what feels natural to you, what feels generous, what feels possible.

Whatever brought you here, whether it was your decision, someone else's, or something that unfolded between you, you have adapted. You have lived through uncertainty. You have reorganised your world. You have seen that you can meet change and remain intact.

From here, the future does not need to be dramatic to be meaningful. It can be shaped around what feels honest and alive to you now. There can be room for joy here. Room for love, in whatever form it takes. Room for a life that fits more comfortably now.

You are no longer standing at the edge of something unresolved. You are living inside the shape of your life as it is now.

real world statistics & trends

optional reading

The following statistics are included for perspective only. Some readers find reassurance in seeing how common these experiences are. Others may prefer to skip this section entirely.

context and scale

1. Marriage rates have declined over time.

In 1960, 72% of American adults were married. By 2020, this figure had fallen to around 50%. [1]

2. Many marriages end in divorce.

An estimated 40–50% of marriages in the United States end in divorce, with higher rates for subsequent marriages. [2]

3. Divorce in midlife and later life has increased.

The divorce rate for adults aged 50 and older doubled between 1990 and 2015. [3]

---

the scale of unpartnered adulthood

4. A large share of adults are unmarried or previously married.

Approximately 117.9 million adults in the United States are divorced, widowed, or have never married. [4]

5. Living without a spouse or partner is increasingly common.

The share of U.S. adults living without a spouse or partner rose from 39% in 2007 to 42% in 2017. [5]

6. Unpartnered adulthood is common across midlife.

Among adults aged 40 to 54, the share living without a spouse or partner increased from 24% in 1990 to 31% in 2019. [6]

---

household structure

7. Single-person households are common worldwide.

Globally, around 13% of households consist of one person, a share comparable to couple-only households without children. [7]

8. Single-parent households represent a significant portion of families.

An estimated 8% of households worldwide are single-parent households. [7]

---

life after separation

9. Many single adults report stable life satisfaction.

Long-term research shows that many adults who remain single report stable life satisfaction across adulthood. [8]

---

references for this book

[1] U.S. Census Bureau. (1960–2020). *Marital Status of the Population*. Decennial Census and American Community Survey.

[2] National Center for Family & Marriage Research. (2018). *Divorce Rate in the United States*. Bowling Green State University.

[3] Brown, S. L., & Lin, I.-F. (2012). *The Gray Divorce Revolution*. Journals of Gerontology: Social Sciences.

[4] U.S. Census Bureau. Current Population Survey. *Marital Status of Adults Aged 18 and Over*.

[5] Pew Research Center. (2018). *The Changing Profile of Unmarried Parents* and related partnership analyses.

[6] Pew Research Center. (2021). *Rising Share of U.S. Adults Are Living Without a Spouse or Partner*. Analysis of U.S. decennial census data and American Community Survey data.

[7] United Nations. (Various years). *World Marriage Patterns* and *Household Composition Reports*.

[8] DePaulo, B. (2014–2020). Analyses of U.S. Census data and longitudinal social survey research on single adulthood and life satisfaction.

assertive rights

a comfort and permission list

- I have the right to take my own inner signals seriously, even when I cannot fully explain them.
- I have the right to change my mind, even after I have tried hard, stayed long, or hoped deeply.
- I have the right to decide that something is no longer workable, without needing a dramatic reason.
- I have the right to leave a commitment that no longer comforts, sustains, or supports my wellbeing.
- I have the right to prioritise my health, safety, and steadiness, even if others are disappointed.
- I have the right to outgrow roles, agreements, or versions of myself that once made sense.
- I have the right to hold complexity without turning it into blame.
- I have the right to take time before knowing what comes next.

- I have the right to remain single for as long as I need, without treating it as a failure or a delay.
- I have the right to acknowledge grief without using it as evidence that I made the wrong choice.
- I have the right to trust my timing, even when it does not match other people's expectations.
- I have the right to make decisions quietly, without consensus or permission.

when the decision was not yours

unexpected endings

Not every separation begins with a private turning. Sometimes the decision is made by the other person. If you are reading this after being left, the internal process described in these pages may feel reversed. Clarity may come later.

There is no single sequence for understanding the end of a relationship. For some, the recognition settles slowly. For others, it arrives abruptly.

If your clarity is unfolding after the separation rather than before it, you are not behind. You are simply starting from a different point.

Take the time you need to understand what has shifted.

acknowledgements

This book is for anyone standing at the edge of a difficult decision, especially those for whom life feels uncertain, fragile, or quietly frightening. If you are a parent carrying the weight of not knowing how things will unfold, I see you. I can't promise that everything will work out neatly, but I can say you are not alone in facing the unknown.

I want to acknowledge **my daughter,** Koda, who continues to teach me what courage looks like in practice. Becoming her parent has sharpened my understanding of what matters, and has reminded me that no amount of compromise is worth losing your peace or your sense of self. I hope she grows up knowing that her needs matter, that her voice matters, and that she never has to become smaller to be loved.

I'm deeply grateful to **my parents** for raising me to believe in myself, even during the seasons when I struggled to hold that belief on my own.

I also want to acknowledge **my younger self.** The part of me that kept noticing, even when I wasn't ready to act. The part that understood, long before I had language for it, that my needs mattered and that I was not responsible for making everyone else comfortable in order to feel safe or worthy of love.

To my three cats, **Mune, Taiko and Whisp,** thank you for being my quiet companions throughout this journey. A special thanks to Taiko, who kept me company for most of this book.

Writing these books has given me a way to sit with what was once unclear or unspoken. Singlehood offered the space to listen more carefully, to take up room again, and to move without rushing. Over time, that has brought a steadier sense of self, not through certainty, but through attention.

> *If there is anything to take from these pages, it is the quiet permission already present. The permission to trust yourself, to move at your own pace, and to let strength grow without needing to announce itself. To choose yourself gently, as an act of care.*

Thank you for being here, and for reading with such honesty.

about author

Jace writes for people who are already paying attention to their inner lives, even when they are unsure what to do with what they notice.

Her work explores singlehood, separation, and emotional autonomy without instruction, urgency, or self-improvement frameworks. She is interested in how people recognise misalignment, how they live through transitions quietly, and how steadiness can return without justification or performance.

Jace is the author of *Dare to be Single* and writes a series of short, recognition-based books designed to reduce pressure rather than create it. Her approach is observational and companionable, offering language for experiences many people already sense but find difficult find to articulate.

She lives in Australia and believes that clarity often arrives slowly, that discomfort can carry information, and that people are allowed to choose peace without needing a dramatic reason.

if you're curious about what comes after

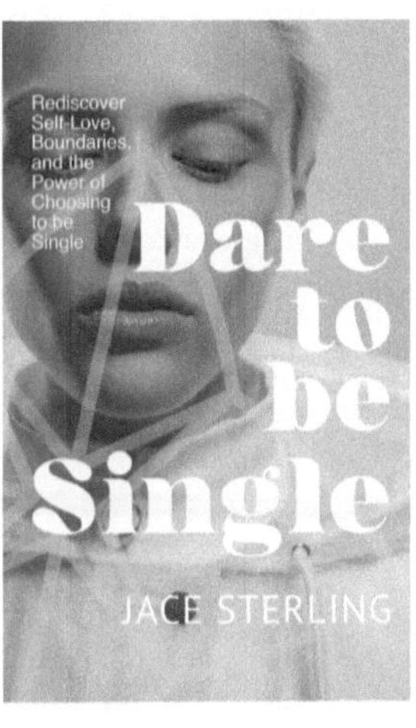

knowing when to leave sits with the moment before and just after truth is acknowledged.

It stays close to uncertainty, misalignment, and the private work of recognising when staying is costing too much. It does not rush resolution or offer a new identity. Its role is to help you trust what you are already noticing.

Dare to be Single was written for a different phase. It begins once the decision has been made, or once singlehood has arrived in your life in a way that is no longer theoretical.

Where this book is about recognising and releasing, *Dare to be Single* is about rebuilding presence, steadiness, and self trust inside singlehood itself.

The tone is more direct. More confronting at times. It speaks plainly about what happens when there is no longer a relationship to orient around, and when you are asked to meet yourself without negotiation, distraction, or permission from anyone else.

Dare to be Single is not a guide to dating, and it is not a manifesto against relationships. It does not promise confidence, glow ups, or reinvention. What it does offer is language, internal dialogue, and grounding practices for learning how to be with yourself again. It includes reflective prompts, self soothing dialogue, and short recognitional pieces designed to interrupt self abandonment and rebuild internal safety.

It is a book for people who want to make the most of singlehood rather than rush through it. For those who want to heal, reset, and understand who they are when no one else is shaping the rhythm of their life.

Some people arrive at *Dare to be Single* immediately after leaving. Others need time before they are ready for its directness. There is no correct sequence and no expectation that you move on quickly. The books are related, but they are not interchangeable.

If *this book* helped you stop overriding yourself, *Dare to be Single* is where the work of standing with yourself truly begins, if and when you feel ready for that step.

You are not required to read it. You are not expected to be there yet.

But when singlehood stops feeling like an aftermath and starts feeling like a space you want to inhabit well, **Dare to be Single** is waiting.

———

" If loving you means abandoning myself, then what

we call love is just mutual imprisonment. True

devotion doesn't ask us to make ourselves smaller;

it invites us both to grow into our fullness."

— JACE STERLING, Dare to be Single